WAITING FOI

GW01260297

Waiting for Trumpets

DAPHNE ROCK

PETERLOO POETS

First published in 1998
by Peterloo Poets
2 Kelly Gardens, Calstock, Cornwall PL18 9SA, U.K.

**A catalogue record for this book is available
from the British Library**

ISBN 1-871471-71-0

Printed in Great Britain by
Latimer Trend & Company Ltd, Plymouth

ACKNOWLEDGEMENTS are due to the editors of the following magazines and in which some of these poems first appeared: *Bound Spiral, Iron, Quartz, Rialto, Staple* and *Spokes*.

For the family

Contents

Flight

Custody sergeant chalked him up all right.
Cell Number Four. Called himself Jones.
A small man, pale, unsteady,
not the full shilling I'd say.
There were four pound coins, a key
in one pocket. A screwdriver.
In his hand, fingers clenched and prised apart
a pigeon feather. He moaned
when we took it so
we bagged it up with the rest
and banged him up, as I said.

I rolled up his socks and poked around.
Bad luck for me, I'd be off soon.
Might catch Tracy, in time, you know,
for a quick one. Nothing in his shoes.
My feather, he muttered, over and over.
When we caged him he stood
arms out, palms up.

Funny one Sarge, I said. Wants his feather.
Sergeant was watching
WDC Mills, he likes to have women around
so long as they don't detect.

I looked in on Jones. Still standing
inspecting his empty hand. Feather, he carried on.
I asked the Sarge, why not
give him his feather back.
Mills giggled and Sarge said, showing off,
so he can bugger himself?

Next time I looked he had flown
on a shirt strip round his neck
and his hands hung down like wings

dropped in mid flight.
I was due off duty, but
death in a cell delays
ordinary rotas. Sarge was concerned to preserve
his chalked up list of checks.
He made some joke about
doing his bird, feathers flying.

He'll make sure
feathers don't fly here.
Funny how I forgot
Tracy, how he put me in mind
of a pheasant hooked to a rail,
like when I was a kid, and mum said,
don't be so daft, boy, it's only a bird.

Bomber Harris

A sky bruised with lightning
as stone cold Bomber Harris
is hoisted out of his box.

Don't worry the skies say,
you're not trapped in a burning cockpit
or pierced with tracer.

No specs smashed into your eyeballs.
Rain slices like shingle
into the ground, wrecking an ants' nest.

You died in your bed says the sky.
Never to plummet into a firestorm,
never to fry in ruins.

Thunder has shifted. Longer gap
between flash and roll.
Bombs away. Going home.

He is twitched into sight,
his blind stone eyes
do not navigate skies.

Ants repair ruined nests
Dresden thrives over bones
unmarried to bodies.

Nothing will marry
that man mapping his flights
with his stone bones and his blank eyes.

Soaked in rain, chipped with hail,
thunderstorms spit in the eye
of stone cold Bomber Harris.

Child Murder

This is a poem for the father of the child murdered in November 1989,
reportedly for not being able to write her name.

You gave me an impossible name,
Sukina. You spent
hours tracing it on your pad,
proving you were
able and in control.

Once you broke a window
when the fly refused to be taught
a lesson in dirty habits,
and it escaped through the star
in the casement.

My school books were yours,
I wrote "e" the wrong way round,
and scrubbed out mistakes.
Your pain was unbearable,
you gave it to me.

I'm dead. You're my daddy
but you are me, and you'll
find your blood
stuck on the shattered star,
smudging my illspelt name.

Changing

Crutch slipping towel over
bobbing white bottoms,
my mother said: "Turn your back to the cave's mouth".
Fighting wet one piece skin
over the thighs,
my mother said: "Someone's coming".
Caught on a toe, peeling the leg elastic through,
but bottoms are rude —
hide the flat chest, hairless groove?
My mother said: "Take a large towel".
Back in the damp, sucking tide-line cave,
knickers on first, sticking,
towel trapped by vest, keep it down, keep it down.
My mother said: "Something is showing".
Button up. I'm decent I said.

Plunge in the pool, hair drifting, breasts drifting.
I'm fifty, I'm naked, I'm decent I said.

Too Many Years in Provence

When she was washing the Volvo in St Jory de Chalais
Monsieur le Curé lifted his hand in blessing
and Madame Leclerc clucked as she sliced les cêpes
and Pascal ran off his first beer of the day
and the tractor churned lime dust over paving
and brooms swept blossom into gutters
and wasps searched for spare baguettes
and buzzards flew through the valley
as she polished wheel hubs and scrubbed
at bird lime crusted on windows.

Marguerite set bread in baskets
and rolled forks in napkins
and filled the Ricard jugs with water

the English madame worked on,
brown thighs tightened and quivered
stretching for dust on the roof rack
washing the Volvo on Sunday
in St Jory de Chalais.

Graveyards in Prague

1. OLD JEWISH CEMETERY

"When you've seen one you've seen 'em all" he said,
telephoto bouncing on his paunch.
He snapped a tear
taking precipitous turns on a ragged face,
and jerked Leah's arm.
"Stand by that pile of slabs to give it scale."
Nice in her pleats and pressed silk
Leah obliged.
"Damn place to small" he said "for a good shot."
He left her among the dead
and tripped on a Star of David.
"Godawful place," he said, "death trap,"
dusting his knees, fitting the lens cap back.
She turned away.
"Dammit Leah, I'm bruised. We have to go."
She looked back as they left,
tasting the tears in her mouth.

2. NEW JEWISH CEMETERY

Under the leaves there are still
chestnuts the air has not dulled.
I have pocketed three for childhood.

Fat women cross the aisles
of chestnuts, knowing their graves,
scraping them clean of leaves.

The seed of the dead here
is pocketed by history,
the stem of Jesse cut.

Names without bones
end genealogies
with Auschwitz, Terezin, or Birkenau.

Saplings flourish
in basalt cracks
but few Jews.

Ave Maria

I'm Mary.
I didn't believe
when I threw up and my breasts swelled sore
and the monthly flow stopped
that I'd fallen.

When I was ten, gossiping in alleys,
I believed you caught it
from the seat in the yard.

My mother said
God sent seed after marriage,
when He chose, soon or late or never.
I thought He'd slipped up,
believed I was wed,
given a gift too soon.

So I told
the gossips, matrons, aunts
God sent the child.
Joseph said, *Is it mine?*
I never knew then
how a child was made.
Joseph said
we'd slipped up, not God.
Explained and confused me
as I was wrapped and hustled from Nazareth.

Such an uncomfortable business
to put a woman through.
How did He choose
bodies for babes — and be everywhere?
Did He use angels?
I saw an angel once
but they said I was proud . . .

Joseph was not pleased,
tired I expect — I could scarcely
carry jugs from the well.
He slept aside from me, snored,
still bothered over the seed
someone had slipped in.

I peered over my belly
at stars stuck up in the sky.
Couldn't believe that God
wasn't the one.
God is not mocked, they said,
but I still don't understand
who slipped up.

Return To Life: Attempted Suicide

1. THE ACT

At the florist
tiger lilies courted you,
on the bookstall
a new Keats gleamed with reviews.

All you could think was
how they were blessed
with an early end.
Their death spoke tongues.

On the street
you did not observe lovers,
children skipping or plump cheeks,
you saw the sunk-in smackhead,
bickering couples, tramps in boxes.

You heard trains scream,
feet drag, hands slap.

We would all have
given our eyes, our ears
for your use
but you were out watching
across the Styx for your deadboat.

2. THE HOSPITAL

You strain on your bonds,
rolling, punching the air,
having freedom cruelly held
beyond reach.

Screens speak to us, no guessing
your mind's path. Your voice
that might plead, let me go, is denied.
You are possessed, not dead.

Your mouth is stuffed with tubes
cuttingly bound to your throat.
Hands, torso, thighs exude
wires like a junction box.

You sentenced yourself to death
and are force fed life.

3. THE OBSERVER

O Persephone I shout, I cup my hands,
offer a draught of warm words
but you are deep in your underworld,
echoes return to ice on my lips.

O Persephone, if you come home
you will be half bound to that dark world.
There will be scars on your lips
like pomegranate seeds.

God in York

1. THE MINSTER

Five Sisters of the North Transept:
thin fingers, shadow long,
pointing up to Zion,
God framed in lead and packed in broken glass:
no pictures here
showing the word, the way.

Five Sisters of the North Transept,
an ill set jigsaw
framed by peasants,
dark as the thirteen hundreds,
light trapped behind
and nicked with leper squints of red and blue.

Five Sisters of the North Transept,
red blue eyes in key holes
piercing the hovel after death,
the diseased eye squinting, pierced
with red blue splinters,
pain now for heaven.

Five Sisters of the North Transept:
gaze assembles
patterns out of fallout, ash, carbon, acid rain.
God's lava dances and preserves
God's small bright eye,
changing, piercing, holding the dark sky.

2. SALVATION ARMY CHAPEL, GILLYGATE

Christ's soldier took up arms here:
General Booth,
"Fire and Blood" stone carved above the door.
This unframed God
picks lice with lepers,
claps to tambourines,
treads blood from stones,
fires hell and lights the sky.

Berlin 1992

1. BRANDENBERGER TOR

Unbolted it is still a frontier . . .
West there are leaves, scurrying from Tiergarten
to lap the Reichstag,
East continues its business, there is space here,
no hurry; the Gate is dwarfed by
Unter den Linden, a brow cleared of furrows,
restored and remade to match the past.
Universitat, Bebelplatz, Bibliotek:
in the West the Topographie des Terrors,
sits in a treeless waste.

Once there were coach parties
threaded with trinkets,
leering at captives
over the wall,
now Zoo belongs to them all.

2. THE WALL IN PIECES

It turns up in packs of three
or in paperweights and keyrings,
stamped genuine, and its colour
fragment of some artistic protest
or martyr's memorial.

It's as if the Sistine Chapel has collapsed
in bits of Michelangelo.

The pieces glow like rubies.
Once entire they split the heart of a city,
they are now split and packaged and
stripped of their core.

The sum of their parts stalks on
ghost wall winding the city
waiting for burial.

3. GHOST STATIONS

It burrowed under Berlin, the invisible wall,
the U-bahn scurried through
dust shrouded stations
entombed in the East.

Now they've been polished,
raised from the dead.
New named for a new time.
No more Lenin-allee.

Alexanderplatz open to all
free to go east or west.
Tread with care, lest old ghosts

drape their shrouds
on invisible walls
and upset your sense of direction.

4. AT THE JEWISH LIFE EXHIBITION

At Walter Gropius Bau
every display
bears witness to race purity.
I read the visitors' heads: how do I know
which boxes to put people in:
Czech, Slav, Bulgarian, Pole,
Bosnian, Serbian, Turk,
Magyar and Azerbayjani.

Do blood tests show
our birthmarks.

I thought I would discover
my own people here.
I have found silverware, menorah,
Yiddish illumination, scrolls and torah,
wall hangings, robes and hats,
Sabbat and Kaddish.

Not blood at all. Not noses and arched eyebrows
not circumcision. Just ways of living,
household gods and props to shore up self
not merely dust and water,
with history I exist.

Props have deserted their owners
and herd in the ghetto
of Walter Gropius Bau.
I must say Kaddish for them
and find new gods.

5. BALCONY POEM

Balconies hang like trapezists
or suicides. They throw down plaster death notes.
A chipped garland, sooty wings from a cherub.
They've lived too long in Berlin
to expect a safety net or Samaritan.

They shrug tired shoulders,
sagging like burst suitcases away from the house.

Some say the Stasi
turned balconies, enlisting them as agents.
In the streets of Prenzlauerberg
death by balcony
is in the ordinary run of hazards.

6. COUNCIL UMBRELLA

The S-Bahn on Schonhausallee
rises on stilts, horror movie spider,
or, as wits remark, the Council Umbrella.
Trains thunder overhead like bombers.
Not forgotten.

You walk in peace on Schonhausallee.
No cursing but greeting. Stalls sell
bright peppers and meats.
At Bornholmstrasse lookouts and guns are gone,
East meets West without a seam.
Only the S-Bahn, pressing overhead
shakes flakes of concrete down, says,
keep your eyes open, remember, this is Berlin.

7. TOURIST TRAP

I pick at this city,
gannet on its tip of spent shells,
its cornucopia of rotten fruit.
An appetite for horror
becomes legitimate.
Careful, careful, there's poison lodged in profane ground,
in walls preserved or destroyed,
in shell holes and scorch marks,
in photographs, films, history books,
poison to turn blood hot for furious deeds.

The past is a dangerous diet
for those who sit comfortably.

Picture on a Hill in Szechuan

Today it is his turn for the water buffalo;
thin arms grip the yoke like pliers.
Bare below the knees his legs paddle the mud.

They move without ripples, stuck to the back-
drop of a slow hill where paddies
fingerprint the earth with whorls of flat water.

It's a photostop for the plush bus.
Tourists tumble to catch their water buffalo,
tearing the picture out for their albums.

And the foreground blur is
the yoke splashing, the thin shirt
trailing his panic leap out of the picture.

The water settles as the yoke
slides down the haunches
and rests.

Pit Death

They mourn the hurtling cage, the bones
poking through skin and dusted black with coal,
lungs scarred and wrecked, they mourn
runaway trucks and voices
crying behind rockfalls,
fading, and soon to be
mute swans on a lignum lake.

There's sickness underground,
black bands for pit death,
and no life after for such skill and sinew.
Slag heaps will slide and bury
towns built on coal,
no thanks and no apology, just
uneconomic. Men who could be freed
to sing, now call for their bonds again.

Clare and Saint Francis

Like Assisi she sat in the sun.
Roman tablets warmed in summer walls
and paving burned underfoot.
She fed on grapes and olives.

One man scorched her. Francis.
She dreamed him as a prince,
as a firefly, as a green oak.
She woke with his ghost in her arms
and he flushed her skin like the sun.
He came naked and with god.

She vexed her father as he vexed his
(throwing his raiment back, denying earthly goods,
unashamed of his skin).
She took off her gold bands, her ceinture,
finger-combed her hair.
Refused her suitors and rejected home.

She knelt to Francis, her head brushing his loins
and he cut her hair,
all her maidenhead in her hair.
Fire pricked her breast and belly.
Her stomach shrank with fasting,
denial his child in her womb.
They married god together.

He heard Assisi buzz
with gossip. So close and never lovers?
He sent her packing. They say
she fell on her knees in the olive grove,
unable to move away.

He preached to birds. He celebrated love
of all creation. Travelled far

and fed on visions. God assured him,
Clare survived on alms.

His blood dripped from stigmata,
her womb dried.

Sea Change

He was a sharp eyed child,
many feet had passed
along this beach and
overstepped the spiral.

On his palm it sat
then tight in his fist
as if warming
might make it jump.

We set it
with cowries and bladder wrack,
sea holly, crab claws,
dribbles of gilt sand.

He's been quieter since,
viewing the treacherous world
that reared its silt
over the ammonite,

smothered it whole;
trusting neither
seas nor tides, nor
parents making light.

For Myra Hindley

I want to say, this is a different moor.
I am not your best guide
to bones and other scraps the hills abound in.

Still-begotten babes, dug in roughly, dead.
Sick mill hands, dropped from long drudging.
Birds, felled by home-made slings,
mice, moulded in owl pellets,
runaways, frosted to roots . . .

Why do you trundle me over old deaths
like a geiger counter.
I have lost the machinery that rings to burial.

Another Way of Life

So you've lain
sixty five years in a Home,
deaf, blind and nearly dumb . . .

I see your head like a peach,
downy, and one ridged stalk
of a neck, lodged in your throat,
your head dense with its flesh,
flesh all through,
no maggotty wisdom, no
labyrinths carved by strangers . . .

You've been
bathed and carried and soothed,
fortunes laid at your feet
by diligent parents.
You've been
a chrysalis trapped in the amber of your flesh;

inside the peach
you do not need wings.

A Not Incest Poem

Rising early I disturbed my father
who had already shaved, made fires
and then sat peacefully on the lavatory
smoking his first Players of the day.

In the kitchen he had his back to me,
shoulders rounded under cotton stripes
and hips full where the folds bunched
from the braided cord.

When he turned he had one hand
clutching the drawstring. The other held
the gaping, deep slit edges tightly lapped.
Rising early, my father did not disturb me.

The Spanish Queen of Hearts

*For Isabelle of Castile, married to Ferdinand of Aragon, under whose
rule Spain became a nation. Her monument is in the Chapel Royale,
Granada, and her sarcophagus lies beneath.*

She is coiffed in marble, every hair in place,
flat out, her back straighter than
it ever was, riding across wild Spain.
She is pure white, flanked by saints,
dues paid and candles lit. She is as sure
and immovable as when
she made the Inquisition, setting the sinless up
as idols to destroy idolators.

Implacable, the cold white hands that do not tremble;
the heart blocked out in stone.

Beneath the floor her body rots in wood:
a domed box, hooped in iron, squeezes her
to little leather strips of curling skin
and bone dust, trickling over paper hair.

Etruscan

We are almost sure of them, we have caught their words in
                    stone chips flying from chisels,
seen their footprints in rivers.

We have peered under Roman pillars where their roots lie,
their names are twisted around our towns.

They tease us like fireflies, dazzle and flit amongst oaks and
                    olives by night,
by day their secrets chatter and gossip to lizards.

Very old, before Rome: we pick at their history with greedy
                    fingers,
holding our blank pages ready to set them in print.

They are wiser than coelacanth, mammoth and bones in African
                    gorges
carbon dated and shredded for knowledge.

They have left us tablets of stone and baffles that block
                    their voices
mocking us.

Second Hand Clothes Shop

This is a shell beach, strewn
with hollow casings.

Swansdown drifts on the dusty bones of a hanger,
shot velvet, cut on the cross, clings flat to a wall,
wrecked ribs touching.
Kid gloves stretch like crab claws.

Camisoles swell with cunning tucks and darts
that plump deceitfully but the breast,
hinted, dissolves
in a handful of crepe de chine.
Shoes gape in pairs
like empty bi-valves.

Sarah says,
will people keep my clothes —
I can't believe it.
She skips out and a stir of air
shivers the stuffs, which sway
then fall back still.

Ducks on the A44

It was a pattern
written on dirt under roads,
the way to water.
She was a duchess
disdaining cars,
neither to right nor left she looked,
leading her ducklings.
Neither to right nor left:
she stepped down the kerb. They followed.
This was an ancient way, a map
in their down heads.
Trucks swerved, brakes bit
as she crossed the A44:
trumpets might have sounded,
cloaks been flung in the mire.
The Red Sea rolled and retreated:
she passed, neck stiff, not knowing
how singly miracles come.

Bulbs

Love took me in November by the heart
and hands that used to plant
spring iris, aconite and scilla;
no time that month to start

trenching the deep, dark, winter burrows,
to drop unpromising brown bulbs
in pits below the sodden earth,
no time to rake the even furrows

for rain drains. So the winter spring
produced no yellow, white and green.
When love relaxed the heart and hand
too late to burrow, dig and fling

corms to the magic soil and rain;
the ground bred rotting vegetation,
prodigal food for worms and thrips.
I'll plant before I love again.

Winter Flowering Cherry

Bad mannered merchandise elbowed the summer out,
burst in without knocking;
tinsel curled in the sun, embarrassed to find itself
draped around beach balls.

Crackers, film wrapped against fading, were
tucked in the early bird's cupboard,
giving off silent mews of boredom.

My flowering cherry
sits modest on the edge of winter,
feeds on her leaf food, grows
tiny cysts stuffed with folded,
not yet pink petals
which will swell and burst
without package or post
to cheer the season.

She will shut up shop
in February.
No need for the crocus
to tread on her heels.

Indian Summer

In this late summer
nasturtiums abseil over falling leaves,
their petal dresses scallopped with frost.

Flowers on the rim of winter
throw off green coats and dance.
Dusk snips the dancers on the outer edge.

The dance has no innocence: passion
disposes this scorched ballet.
I too will spend my late days blazing.

Waiting for Trumpets

Norton Church, Radnor

She plays inexpertly
hymns in an empty church,
hidden behind
a swag of dahlias and marguerites.

He mows between graves.
This one was ten
at the time of Waterloo:
beloved wife survived for twenty years.

He leaves a bicycle
unsecured by the lych-gate;
jacket folded on a weathered stone,
it holds shape, plump and quick.

It's full of Partridges,
this aviary of forebears facing west
and lichen carving
new fancies on beautitudes.

He shaves the dead close,
his two-stroke antiphon to treble pipe.
Partridges stare blankly west,
waiting for trumpets.

Time to Shut the Doors

After weeks of waking to
dawn tripping up dusk,
walls lined with leaf shadow
sun beating blinds . . .

after butterflies losing track
between building and branches,
slip of toes on grass,
rings bleached on fingers . . .

after all it has rained . . .

and I'm tucking up flesh,
looking out lentils,
stuffing cracks with blankets

. . . the spider spins
a winter coat of wasps,
worms put on leaves like gloves
the sun shortcuts its way across the sky . . .

time to plant myself like a bulb
and sit out the dark.

Bees

I would like to dwell briefly on bees
which pursue sweet and secret ways
amongst their acolytes.

Postulant flowers
stripe and tint and blush,
ribbon and paint,
perfume, twine and tumble wantonly.

Bees have shown voluptuous joy this year,
purring and gathering
from passion flowers which burst
in huge rococo buds, their jewelled crosses
hung on purple haloes,
set in white surplices with topaz beads.

Chickweed thrives too,
its pinhead blooms of washed-out white
furnishing jamjar altars.

I would like to sit in a bee's brain
pondering the antics of flowers.

A Village Stone Mason

We store secrets in our fingers, we who carve
white stone into angels and virgins
leaning from roof and clerestory.

Down to earth
these women back their men up
with soup and cabbage; unaware
of their images high over altars
lips dashed with cherry and breasts white.

My Alisoun has a dun skin and cracked lips.
She's an angel with pastry but
no match for Mary
whose breasts have served the lord.
My Alisoun smells, her fingernails are black
and she's round on the hip,
lopsided, having toted bairns
one by one. She overflows our pew.

Fined down, chipped to perfection,
she was my only model. My single breast and thigh.
Who else would grace a mason hired to sculpt
such intimacies.
In darkness under blankets
my secret hands
match her curves to angels.

Some Questions About the Woman Taken in Adultery

How did they? Was it
a tip-off, whispers over the inn table?
Perhaps he was bored, betrayed her
or, if she was pregnant, got out
while the going was good,
as they say.

You can bet half a dozen
already knew, admired, clapped him
on his back, you dog!
Her friends may have wished her well,
shivering, half appalled,
knowing the law.

No mention of him in the script.
I suppose they dragged her
off him, kicking and screaming,
Jezebel temptress, Lilith corrupter of flesh,
stones itched to be hurled
from hands she had denied.

The voice, moral and just,
piercing their frenzy, so that
they stood still, let him without sin
cast the first stone. They considered
how little sin came their way,
they had not lain with her.

All the same, he should not be ignored,
they said he did miracles, cured
some very nasty diseases —
might need to call on him
some time, better drop the stones,
keep on the right side.

Where did she go then?
Clutching a blanket one old goodwife
had thrown to cover those pink pearls.
Did he draw up a care plan,
find her a refuge, offer
stress counselling?

Or was she pursued through the dust
after he left, bare feet stone cut
in her stumble after hope
of mass conversion
while they renewed vengeance
according to law, bringing her down.

Deconsecrated

He does not speak
and no-one waits for his voice.
God is banished,
they have
asperged his stone shell
to bar his right of way.

There were mysteries,
magic and marvels,
sleight of hand.
Wine became blood.
One angel sinned and fell
and went out raging.

God goes quietly
(the drama always unfolded
after he left)
already the stage
is cleared of his tricks
filled with theirs,

cardboard stairs, doors into
illusory gardens,
rooms with three sides,
fires without heat,
tea without taste,
flat turrets and towers.

Both share
periods of dark
when legerdemain is worked,
inflating souls
with angel dust
to keep them aloft.

Lightning Strike

Stark wide, its boughs like arms
without kin. Main trunk
still wrapped in bark, but thinner shoots
have lost their leaders, stare
white naked, stiff limbs spread
shocked against the sky.

Beside this burnt out frame
an oak whose sprigs
peel stipules back from buds
to clothe the winter shape in green and gold
under whose bark
sap runs already quick to feed the spring.

The old tree stands,
print from a bombed landscape,
crutched body frozen in mid frame,
black fingers charred: stuck to the sky,
a smile stretched on black lips
stark as the barren branch
with all her children gone.

Those Church Halls

At seven after dark lights spring up
in church hall windows, lights
more yellow than at home
or in streets.

Inside there will be
stuffy cloakrooms and girls cautious with rouge,
girls whose eyes remain
bluish with childhood.

They will wear
good grey cardigans,
and bunch their beauty
under pleats and gathers.

Their hearts' beating will disturb
pin tucked blouses,
wild girls beneath decorum,
waiting for magic.

That was before
childhood retreated, before
fashion, ungentle, bared
too tender flesh:

yellow lit halls still shine,
but the girls
are now too young for breasts;
the oldest are elsewhere

in Miss Selfridge black, pretending
they have dipped deep
with no strange country left
for wild imagining.

Batlight

Someone has thrown
a handful of dust at the sun,
tree shapes blur
and light is stirred up
like muddy water,

then the pipistrelle
tunes up his minute violin,
his night's work dawning.

Between mote and shade
lepidoptera dance
to his tune

his pleated wings
unfold and rehearse
elliptical themes

which arrange his prey
into notes and bars,
he slips their chorales
deep into the dark
of his hunger.

Historical Map

My treaties, congresses, my routs,
my last stands, sieges, glorious first,
retreats and melancholy losses . . .

a private army roll, here is
no Gallipoli nor Flodden Field,
Normandy, Pearl Harbour, Mafeking,

nowhere of note. My places are as mild
as Gallipoli before men died there,
you would be surprised to find
battle trophies on these heaths
or in cold coves
where sand is twice renewed
each day; but I will give you names
like Mewslade Bay, Box Hill, like Farthing Down,
Three Cliffs and Roker Park,
places for treasure hunters where
metals underground set off alarms,
and searchers find thinned bone
where wedding rings once burrowed into flesh;
all kinds of rusty bounty mark my map
my map of good fights, yes.

The X-Ray Album

These pictures
do not set her against
trees or household gods.
Pure body trimmed to the rib edge;
they penetrate the skin
to light up bone and tissue.

The doctors have seen things
(not to be handled by patient)
they have turned her inside out
and matched their knives to blueprints
while she slept.

She dreams of heads bent,
gloves probing her cavities,
snipping and darning.
She dreams of a fungus,
candyfloss on the bone,
pitting the bone.

She wakes stitched,
pictures she will never see
locked under her skin.

At the Surgery

She is young and frank,
up to the minute.
Has drugs off by the yard and is
quick to assess me:
born pre-NHS and used to
making do with aspirin.

She is bright with reservations.
Checks. I'm afraid
your cervix has shrunk back,
no hope of a sample.
I picture it. Once supple
as the exuberant children
came through like dolphins.
Now in retreat and brittle:
old glue left in the tube too long.

She continues. No need to fret.
Almost no-one dies
with cervical cancer after sixty-five.
It grows too slow.

For once time is on my side.
I step back into knickers,
hiding the evidence.
Her last shot stings:
sexually active? I am inclined
to irony. What! With a cervix shrunk
no man is long enough,
but bite it back, and
am bright with reservations.

Tideline

1.
In winter I blow dust from bowls of shell
and wash dull stones;
amber veins are relit
in the pebble heart.

Bowls of shell and stone,
all over the house
too old to age.

Odd, employing the empty bivalve
to fill spaces in memory,
rolling the pebble into
cold mornings, brave rush
into breakers and tough seas,
odd, using chips of ammonite,
themselves sarcophagi . . .

2.
All over the beach there were children
with hands full of pearl thrown up after the storm

pockets emptied over the sink,
damp sand in caverns and spirals,
seas roaring

spine stripped heart urchins
cracked at a touch,
and a pink fingernail shell
its elipse shattered . . .

3.
We throw back shells tight shut with occupants,
collect dead things,
things that will stand still
whose clock has stopped,

shells stuck with curls of
dry seaweed, pallid brown
like hair curled inside lockets,

egg cases blowing like beach balls, and
the Mermaid's Purse dried crisp,
all spawn hatched out;

false jewels that water creates,
fools' gold . . .

4.
There are children all over the house,
running in, pockets full of treasure,
in and out, leaving their prizes behind.
This winter again
I tidy up, I hear the sea roar.